Table of Contents

Greenhouse 3

Advantages of greenhouses : 4

The History of Greenhouses 6

TYPES OF GREENHOUSES..9

Free-standing Greenhouses 11

Gutter-connected Greenhouses 12

Production Systems 12

Building Your Greenhouse 13

Preparing the soil 13

Purchasing the greenhouse..14

Construction of the greenhouse and additional work .. 14

GREENHOUSE LOCAL SITE..16

Topography...17

Microclimate...18

Irrigation and water supply 18

WATER QUALITY FOR CROP PRODUCTION.....................20

Electricity...22

Soil characteristics..22

Pollution..22

Availability of space...23

Availability of labour...23

Infrastructures..23

Orientation...23

Greenhouse Preparation and Scouting...........................24

Pest Management in Greenhouses Using Biological Control
....25

PROPER USE OF PESTICIDES......................................28

Delaying Pesticide Resistance.....................................28

Preventing Pesticide Damage to Plants (Phytotoxicity)....29

Crops That Can Be Planted In A Green House System......30

Crops and their categories...34

Crops That Aren't Suited To a Greenhouse 36

Greenhouse

Greenhouse farming is an agricultural management system that has demonstrated its efficiency in intensifying food production. These systems constitute a feasible alternative for ensuring food supply, which is one of the greatest challenges faced by humankind in the twenty-first century. Technology has been able to meet the challenges related to greenhouse farming in both contributing.

A greenhouse (also called a glasshouse, or, if with sufficient heating, a hothouse) is a structure with walls and roof made chiefly of transparent material, such as glass, in which plants requiring regulated climatic conditions are grown. These structures range in size from small sheds to industrial-sized buildings. A miniature greenhouse is known as a cold frame. The interior of a greenhouse exposed to sunlight becomes significantly warmer than the external temperature, protecting its contents in cold weather.

Many commercial glass greenhouses or hothouses are high tech production facilities for vegetables, flowers or fruits. The glass greenhouses are filled with equipment including screening installations, heating, cooling, lighting, and may be controlled by a computer to optimize conditions for plant growth. Different techniques are then used to evaluate optimality degrees and comfort ratio of greenhouses, such as air temperature, relative humidity and vapour-pressure deficit, in order to reduce production risk prior to cultivation of a specific crop.

Advantages of greenhouses :

• The yield may be 10-12 times higher than that of out door cultivation depending upon the type of greenhouse, type of crop, environmental control facilities.

• Reliability of crop increases under greenhouse cultivation.

• Ideally suited for vegetables and flower crops.

• Year round production of floricultural crops.

• Off-season production of vegetable and fruit crops.

• Disease-free and genetically superior transplants can be produced continuously.

• Efficient utilisation of chemicals, pesticides to control pest and diseases.

• Water requirement of crops very limited and easy to control.

• Maintenance of stock plants, cultivating grafted plant-lets and micro propagated plant-lets.

• Hardening of tissue cultured plants

• Production of quality produce free of blemishes.

• Most useful in monitoring and controlling the instability of various ecological system.

• Modern techniques of Hydroponic (Soil less culture), Aeroponics and Nutrient film techniques are possible only under greenhouse cultivation.

Do you think that greenhouses are a relatively new idea? You probably haven't thought much about it one way or the other.   If you didn't like history in high school, (or even if you did) read on and you will be able to regale your friends with your knowledge of greenhouses from the time of the Romans until today.

The idea of growing plants in environmentally controlled areas has existed since Roman times. The Roman emperor Tiberius ate a cucumber-like vegetable daily. The Roman gardeners used artificial methods (similar to the greenhouse system) of growing to have it available for his table every day of the year. Cucumbers were planted in wheeled carts which were put in the sun daily, then taken inside to keep them warm at night. The cucumbers were stored under frames or in cucumber houses glazed with either oiled cloth known as specularia or with sheets of selenite (a.k.a. lapis specularis), according to the description by Pliny the Elder.

Before the 20th century - Agriculture production inside protected structures was initiated in France and Netherlands in the 19th century. This method was applied in simple, low, glass structures, which provided climate protection, and were used mainly for the growth of ornamental plants.

Modern Times - By the beginning of the 20th century, mostly after the end of 2nd world war, the technology of greenhouse construction accelerated its development, especially in Western Europe cold countries, Netherlands leading the course. Agro-technical systems, aeration solutions and accompanying accessories were gradually added to the structures, while the structure foundations improved to the known, traditional heavy steel constructions covered by rigid glass boards.

New Materials - By the end of the 50ties of the 20th century the greenhouses technology flowed to the north and center of Europe, extending its influence and benefits to Israel, where

a wave of experiments and research in the field had begun. The 60ties revealed a new kind of structure covering sheets. They were the flexible, low priced polyethylene sheets, which caused a conceptual revolution in the field of greenhouses. Simultaneously appeared other types of good light transition coverings, such as polycarbonate (a kind of covering made of plastic polymers) leaving behind the traditional glass covering.

New Technologies - The method of modular structures (Lego-like method) leads to the development of growth technologies suitable for most types of crops, thus creating customized structure projects, customer-tailored according to specific needs. This new trend caused the breakdown of the traditional, conservative Dutch hegemony ruling until then in the field of greenhouses. Nowadays, light-weighted structures with covering made of flexible polyethylene or stiff-flexible polycarbonate are more common and widespread than the mythological rigid glass greenhouses.

TYPES OF GREENHOUSES

A greenhouse is a structure with a glass or plastic roof and side walls that is used for the production of ornamentals and food crops and may be used seasonally or year round. The closed environment of a greenhouse has its own unique requirements, compared with outdoor production. Pests and diseases, and extremes of heat and humidity, have to be controlled, and irrigation is necessary to provide water. Significant inputs of heat and light may be required, particularly with winter production of warm-weather crops.

Greenhouses for commercial production can be classified as free-standing or gutter-connected.

A free-standing greenhouse can have a quonset (hoop), gothic or gable roof shape. The Quonset is usually the least expensive and is available in widths up to 36'. Gothic designs have higher light transmission and shed snow easier. Gable designs may use trusses to span a width up to 60'.

A gutter-connected greenhouse is a series of trusses connected together at the gutter level. Individual bays vary in width from 12' to 25' and have a clearance of 8' to 16' to the gutter. Bays can be put together to get any width of greenhouse desired.

Greenhouses can be made any length. Standard lengths that utilize glazing materials to advantage are 96' and 144'. All greenhouses are modular with frame spacing of 4' or 5' for hoophouses and 10' or 12' for gutter-connected designs.

Most greenhouses are built of galvanized steel tubing and are available from many manufacturers throughout the U.S. Steel makes a strong frame to carry snow and wind loads and still allow about 80% of the light to enter.

Most greenhouses are covered with a plastic glazing. Low-cost polyethylene film or covering applied as an air inflated double cover will last 4 years. Anti-drip agents and infra-red inhibitors are added to give better service and reduced heat loss. Semi-rigid structured sheets of polycarbonate or acrylic are more permanent and have a life of at least 15 years. Tempered glass is used for crops requiring high light levels.

The following is a short review of the advantages of the different styles of structures:

Free-standing Greenhouses

• Easier to provide separate environments as each house is controlled by its own heating/cooling system. One house can be run warm for propagation and the next one, cooler for growing.

• Individual houses can be shut down for periods when not in use saving energy.

• Best suited for heavy snow areas as multi-span houses need heat to melt snow from the gutters.

• Good for non-level sites.

• Individual houses are easier to build and maintain.

Gutter-connected Greenhouses

• More cost effective for areas greater than 20,000 sq ft.

• Reduced heating costs as surface area to floor area ratio is less. Heating costs can be as much as 25% less due to reduced glazed area.

• Less land is needed. About 30% more growing space can be placed on the same amount of land area.

• Heat can be centralized.

• Open-roof designs that eliminate fans and reduce electricity use are available.

Production Systems

In addition to the greenhouse style, there are a variety of production systems used inside the greenhouse. Some crops are grown in containers on benches, such as many spring ornamental crops, while others are grown in the soil in the ground such as cut flowers or vegetable crops (i.e. tomatoes, lettuce). Some crops are grown in containers or bags of growing media that are placed on the ground (tomatoes). Some greenhouses have soil or gravel floors, some have concrete floors and some have a combination. All of these differences contribute to best management practices that will vary according to the greenhouse and systems used for production.

Building Your Greenhouse

Preparing the soil

Once you have decided where to build the greenhouse and determined its size, you will need to prepare the ground surface. First, you need to remove all scrub, bushes and trees. Then you need to level the ground so the surface is even and no bumps or holes remain. Next, you need to take exact measurements of the site and mark the precise position of the greenhouse with spikes.

Now you can start plowing the earth and simultaneously adding fertilizers. You can use natural dried manure as a fertilizer. Alternatively, you can buy organic fertilizers such as dehydrated pellets made from organic cattle or chicken manure. These are more convenient and cleaner to use, transport and disperse.

Purchasing the greenhouse

After having determined the dimensions of the plot and greenhouse (based on its anticipated capacity and output) with your agronomist, you will need to collect price quotes from greenhouse suppliers. You will also need to clarify what materials should be used and what equipment will be required based on what you will plant. This section focuses on using plastic sheeting which is cheaper, safer and easier to install than glass.

Collect information on greenhouses from other greenhouse farmers. Avoid small scale producers who may see you as competition. Other sources for information on greenhouses are the agricultural chamber and agricultural agencies at national and/or local levels. Agricultural consultants are also an excellent source of information because they do not have conflict of interest in providing you advice, but you will need to pay for their services.

Construction of the greenhouse and additional work

Someone will need to be appointed to provide full-time supervision of the construction. This person must have the supplier's contact details, final offer and related documents.

Plan for large vehicles, machinery and workers to access the construction site. If direct access is not possible, arrange with neighbors to let the construction crews use their land to access your plot. It is imperative to agree on access to the construction site prior to signing a contract.

In monitoring the construction, follow the implementation plan, ensuring that work is completed on schedule. If the greenhouse is being built in late winter or early spring, you will need to plant crops immediately after it is completed as delaying can postpone cultivation and harvesting, impacting sales and revenue. This is a higher risk if you have a contract with a wholesaler to supply produce by a certain date.

Once the greenhouse is completed, you and the agronomist should carefully inspect it before signing final delivery forms. Verify that the greenhouse is built according to specifications, and all machinery/equipment is installed and working. Insist that the company rectify any variation from the contract before making the final payment.

You might need a fence around your greenhouse to keep out animals. Animals can eat crops or contaminate them with urine, feces and diseases. If your plot is near a town or otherwise inhabited land, rats and other vermin can cause considerable damage, and you may need to install a special fence to keep them out.

Additional work may be necessary depending on location, type of greenhouse, and which crops will be grown. These additional works need to be planned when developing the business plan and deciding on what crops to grow. If possible, get the greenhouse supplier to include these works in its overall offer, or you will need to engage a separate contractor.

GREENHOUSE LOCAL SITE

The specific selection of a greenhouse location must take into account a variety of factors described below. A GREENHOUSE represents a major investment in the development of your garden, not just from the practical standpoint of being able to grow the plants that you always dreamed of, but also in terms of the effect it will have on the design and appearance of your garden. There is so much to think

Topography

In principle, the location must be flat in width direction, with a slope in the main axes between 0 and 0.5 percent, and never over 1–2 percent, as this would require terracing. In some cases, however, a south-oriented inclined plot (in the Northern Hemisphere) may be acceptable if the chosen greenhouse type adapts well; in this case, mechanization is rare (such as on Spain's south coast, where low-cost greenhouses are common on the coastal slopes – Plate 7). Normally, on steep terrains, it is recommended to build several separate greenhouses with axes parallel to contour lines. Provisions must be made for the evacuation of rainfall water, and greenhouses should not be situated in hollow lands.

As with liquids, cold air moves downwards (as it is heavier than hot air) to the lower parts of the site, and stays there if there is no wind to carry it away. Therefore, it is essential that the local topography is suitable for effective drainage of cold air during calm nights. Frequently foggy areas should be avoided. Areas that are well illuminated and free from shadows (hills, buildings) are preferred. Sites should be protected from cold winds (usually from the north in the Northern Hemisphere), using windbreaks or taking advantage of the topography. If snow is to be expected, greenhouses must be positioned sufficiently far from trees or other obstacles to the wind, since snow may accumulate around such obstacles.

Drip irrigation systems are very cost-effective and save water. They are easy to install and can be rearranged when crop planting changes. Damaged parts can easily be replaced.

Collecting rainwater is the cheapest way to irrigate crops. If community homes or a day center is located next to the greenhouse, rainwater can be collected from the roof and stored in large plastic barrels next to the house, or in concrete tanks dug into the ground. For a large greenhouse, you might consider constructing a large open-air concrete basin for water. Ensure that all water is filtered prior to using it for irrigation.

If you purchase second-hand plastic barrels, ensure that you clean them before use to avoid contaminating the water with chemicals. Though the barrels may seem large, water is used quickly during dry months. It works well to install several barrels connected with hoses. The barrels should be elevated about ½ meter from the ground so the water pressure pushes water through the hose and irrigation pipes without the need for electric pumps. This way, rain water can be used for drip irrigation systems at a minimum cost. Note that underground concrete tanks and open-air basins require electric pumps.

During dry spells you can connect your irrigation system to the municipal water supply or order water to be delivered by truck. In either case, you will need to store the water in your existing water tanks. It is best to let the water stand for a few days before using it to allow

Another source of water is from ground wells. A well provides an abundant and cheap source of water. When digging new, or deepening existing, wells, consult a specialist who will advise on how deep a well needs to be to provide enough water. A well that is too shallow can dry out in summer when demand for water is at a peak and ground water levels are lowest. Ensure that all administrative requirements/permits are obtained prior to drilling to avoid legal disputes. You may need to buy a concession from the municipality to access groundwater. Such concessions, combined with the actual cost of drilling, can amount to significant expenses that must be foreseen in the business plan.

WATER QUALITY FOR CROP PRODUCTION

Irrigation water quality is a critical factor for production of greenhouse crops. There are many factors which determine water quality. Among the most important are alkalinity, pH and soluble salts. But there are several other factors to consider, such as whether hard water salts such as calcium and magnesium or heavy metals that can clog irrigation systems or individual toxic ions are present. In order to determine this, water must be tested at a laboratory that is equipped to test water for irrigation purposes.

Poor quality water can be responsible for slow growth, poor aesthetic quality of the crop and, in some cases, can result in the gradual death of the plants. High soluble salts can directly injure roots, interfering with water and nutrient uptake. Salts can accumulate in plant leaf margins, causing burning of the edges. Water with high alkalinity can adversely affect the pH of the growing medium, interfering with nutrient uptake and causing nutrient deficiencies which reduce plant health.

Reclaimed water, runoff water, or recycled water may require reconditioning before use for irrigation since disease organisms; soluble salts and traces of organic chemicals may be present.

Water quality should be tested to ensure it is acceptable for plant growth and to minimize the risk of discharging pollutants to surface or ground water.

Electricity

Modern greenhouses have temperature, wind and humidity sensors, and automatically regulate inside temperature by elevating and lowering panels. Groundwater wells and underground water tanks need pumps, and storage facilities may need lighting and other climate regulators. Sockets may need to be installed in the greenhouse to power electric tools. If electric cables are installed underground, their exact location needs to be marked on architectural drawings and blueprints of the property.

Soil characteristics

Whether cultivation is directly in the soil or in pots or containers, the soil must have properties appropriate for horticultural crops.

Pollution

For greenhouses located in urban areas, air pollution conditions must be evaluated, not only in terms of incidence on the plants themselves, but also with regard to residues deposited on the greenhouse, which can limit solar radiation (e.g. dust from factories) or damage the greenhouse cladding material.

Availability of space

Space may be required for future enlargement, auxiliary facilities (e.g. water basins for collection of rainfall water or storage of irrigation water) and buildings (e.g. handling, stores, offices).

Availability of labour

If local labour is not available, it is necessary to consider the costs inherent in acquiring labour.

Infrastructures

Proximity to transport networks (e.g. roads, railway), access to communication systems (e.g. telephone, internet) and availability of energy (e.g. gas, electricity) must all be considered.

Orientation

The position must be chosen to avoid shadows from hills or neighbouring buildings. It is necessary to adapt the shape and slope of the roof to dominant winds, while maintaining the objective of maximum light in the greenhouse.

Greenhouse Preparation and Scouting

Before introducing a crop into a greenhouse it is imperative to remove weeds, algae, "pet plants," and any plant and growing medium debris located throughout the greenhouse, particularly underneath benches, because these provide refuge for arthropod pests. In addition, repair any drainage problems that may contribute to recurring arthropod pest outbreaks.

Crops growing in adjacent greenhouses or outdoors should be recorded. Previous pest problems in the greenhouse and current pesticide application methods should be reviewed. A plan of action may then be developed to eliminate these problems prior to the arrival of the crop. Prevention of key pest problems may be more easily accomplished if the grower and scout take the time to identify, analyze and correct problems before crops are introduced. Also, consider how the variety of plants to be grown in the same area may influence ease of pesticide applications and spread of disease. For example, keep seedling and cutting geraniums separate to help minimize spreading bacterial blight. Keep propagation houses separate from other growing areas, and vegetable transplants separate from ornamentals to help reduce the incidence of Impatiens Necrotic Spot Virus when western flower thrips are present.

Pest Management in Greenhouses Using Biological Control

Greenhouses provide a suitable environment (e.g., temperature and light) for numerous biological control agents or natural enemies including parasitoids, predators, and entomopathogenic nematodes. Many natural enemies are commercially available and can be incorporated into existing greenhouse pest management programs. In general, the use of biological control is most effective in extended cropping systems such as cut flowers and vegetables, however they are also being successfully used in short term ornamental cropping systems such as annual bedding plants. Biological control is much easier to implement in a monoculture (single crop) than in a polyculture (multiple crops).

Natural enemies cannot be used in the same manner as pest control materials (insecticides or miticides). Pest control materials are typically applied after arthropod pests reach damaging levels, and when effective, the designated pest control material reduces the arthropod pest population. Using natural enemies as a curative control is less successful compared to applying them preventively. Natural enemies should be released early in the cropping cycle when plants are small, arthropod pest populations are low, and before crop damage occurs. Releases of natural enemies may be required throughout the growing season in order to sustain arthropod pests at low populations.

A biological control program can succeed if these recommendations are followed:

1) Correctly identify all arthropod pests,

2) Purchase natural enemies from a reliable biological control supplier,

 3) Make sure there is a consistent supply of high quality natural enemies,

4) Emphasize that proper shipping procedures be followed, and

5) Obtain directions from biological control suppliers on proper release rates and timing of application.

Start any new biological control program in a small isolated greenhouse, in propagation houses, or in a greenhouse where edible crops such as herbs are being grown. This approach allows you to gain experience and then have the opportunity to expand into other production areas. It is critical to implement a scouting program and establish a favorable relationship with your biological control supplier early. The success of any biological control program relies on patience and a strong commitment to detail (e.g., scouting and record-keeping).

Arthropod pest identification is extremely important when initiating biological control programs in greenhouses because natural enemies, particularly parasitoids, are specific in the types of insect pests they use as hosts. For example, the aphid parasitoid Aphidius colemani attacks both the melon/cotton aphid (Aphis gossypii) and the green peach aphid (Myzus persicae), but does not attack the foxglove aphid (Aulacorthum solani).

PROPER USE OF PESTICIDES

Before using pesticides, obtain the proper training.

Delaying Pesticide Resistance

To use fewer pesticides, it is important that pesticides, when used, are effective at killing pests. Pests can become resistant to pesticides making the pesticide ineffective for management.

Resistance is genetic in nature, and an insect or mite cannot become resistant or acquire resistance during its life (that is, within one generation). Resistance is stimulated by widespread application of a pesticide but some individual pests survive and pass on genetic factors to the next generation. A chemical cannot adjust in response to genetic changes in the pest population that help the pest survive the chemical application. Thus, the surviving pests can transfer the resistance factor(s) into the population, allowing the population to become resistant over a period of time. Repeat applications with one type of pesticide eventually remove almost all the susceptible individuals from a pest population and leave only those with the resistant gene. Pests can become resistant to insecticides to which they have never been exposed. This can happen when two insecticides have a similar mode of action. Mode of Action (MoA) is how a pesticide specifically kills a pest. If two (or more) insecticides attack the pest in the same way, a resistance mechanism to one insecticide may also provide resistance to the other, even though the pest may never have been exposed to that second insecticide.

Preventing Pesticide Damage to Plants (Phytotoxicity)

- Apply pesticides during the cooler part of the day, such as the early morning or evening. Treatments made in the early morning allow foliage to dry before temperatures reach 85–90°F. Take special precautions when using pesticides containing oil. Treat when conditions allow plants to dry quickly.

- Add surfactants only when recommended on the pesticide label.
- Avoid tank mixes. A mixture of insecticides may increase the chance of injury to plants.
- Never use a sprayer for insecticides that was previously used to apply herbicides.
- Apply pesticides only after crops have been irrigated and show no signs of moisture stress.
- Do not use more than one emulsifiable concentrate in a tank mixture.
- Do not apply pesticides with a fertilizer.
- Never use broad-leaved weed killers and brush killers around the greenhouse.

Crops That Can Be Planted In A Green House System

1. Leafy greens are one of the most exciting opportunities for greenhouse produce, particularly the salad types and Bibb lettuces. Nearly all leafy greens will thrive in the same growing environments required

for most ornamental crops, especially bedding plants. Therefore, aside from learning the growing techniques of leafy greens, whether in soil or hydroponics, little adjustment is needed by the ornamental industry to grow leafy veggies. The profitability can be excellent as long as sales are local and as direct to the consumer as possible. The types of greens covers a very wide range of colors, shapes and taste. Today, it is much more than just head lettuce.

2. Microgreens are very popular in restaurants. The types and flavors of microgreens are enormous. One can design different mixes of greens to provide different flavors for different food dishes. An example of different microgreens are Persian cress, Tatsoi, mustards, Pac Choi, radish, Shungiku, Amaranth, beet, Orach, etc. The future is incredible!

3. Spinach is another leafy green that has great possibilities. When grown and sold locally, it offers freshness and good taste. Grown in greenhouses it is clean, free of debris, dirt and excellent from a food safety standpoint. As a greenhouse crop it does tend to

bolt, or go to seed, quite early depending on growing conditions and day length.

4. Cucumbers are popular. The long green cucumbers are more familiar greenhouse varieties for most consumers, but can be a little more difficult to produce, as they need to be shrink wrapped after harvest to keep them firm and fresh. A better choice for greenhouse growers may be the Beit alpha types that are really catching on. I call them "little snackers." These small cukes are easy to package and don't require shrink wrapping as do the long European types. The Beit Alpha types are tender, sweet and seedless–perfect for packing into school lunches.

5. Tomatoes are the most familiar and most common greenhouse vegetable crop, and there are many different options available in all colors, shapes and sizes. Cherries, grapes, tomatoes on the vine (or TOV), and beefsteaks are all popular options. Many growers I work with have been focusing on beefsteak varieties, since the TOV varieties are popular with some of the very largest growers that dominate the market.

6. Peppers have been another popular greenhouse crop. Americans love peppers and there are many types to choose from. Greenhouse bell types of peppers need exact humidity and temperature control, especially the varieties from Holland. They are excellent tasting but are probably the most difficult greenhouse crop to grow. However, there are numerous other types of peppers of all shapes, colors and flavors. One day soon, pepper plants will be sold as edible ornamentals, offering beauty in the home and may also be used to flavor many food dishes. Even with these production challenges, peppers should be a highly marketable crop. Multiple colors of peppers in a clamshell are irresistible.

7. Numerous herbs are available which can be packaged in many ways, with or without the roots. Basil, water cress, cilantro and many others are rapidly being discovered by greenhouse growers. Such crops have a great future in farm markets where sales can be direct to the consumer, allowing freshness and superb quality.

8. Green beans, grown in greenhouses, are in high demand, especially in the inner city, selling for

incredible prices. Again, a variety of colors are available, along with different shapes and lengths. This is a great crop for direct sales to the consumer at farm markets.

9. Swiss chard and squash are great possibilities for greenhouse production if sold directly to the consumer. As with most vegetable crops, these two vegetables come in all shapes and colors.

10. Raspberries and strawberries, grown in greenhouses, are just around the corner. If grown and served with shortcake on the production site, it is a winner. It's a big deal at Wimbledon, why not as part of one's offering at a farm market? The very best tasting strawberries must be red throughout and not shipped in from thousands of miles away. The tastiest are very perishable but offer great opportunities when served on site.

Crops and their categories.

Category Best Plants - Easy to grow

• Tomatoes

• Strawberries

• Squash

• Beans and peas

• Broccoli

• Leafy greens—spinach, kale, arugula and micro greens

• Herbs

• Artichoke

High-producing

• Lettuce and leafy greens

• Cucumber

• Rocket

• Greens

• Beans

* Strawberries

Flowers • Orchids

• Sunflowers

• Cosmos

• Marigold

• Zinnias

• Black-eyed Susan

Ornamentals • Succulents

• Cacti

Crops That Aren't Suited To a Greenhouse

Though most plants grow well in a controlled setting such as in a greenhouse, there are definitely some that are not best suited for one. And, there are also crops that need wind pollination such as wheat, corn, oats, rice, barley and rye. Or, those that need direct or full sunlight such as carrots, rutabaga and radish. These can still be grown in a greenhouse; you'll just need to make sure you give them the conditions they need to thrive.

Category Best plants

Cold frame needed • Carrots

• Some types of herbs

Wind pollinated • Wheat

• Corn

• Oats

• Rice

• Barley

• Rye

Needs full or direct sunlight

• Carrots

• Rutabaga

• Radish